DEDICATION

For my late sister, Celeste
and her son, Dan

****

Rocketing in like a comet
You breached our atmosphere
Full of dazzle and delight
Luminous vibration
We could not hold you
Shooting through celestial space
you left us
Glittering trails of all that was
and could ever be
your too soon departed spirit.

CHAPTER I

THE OAKS

It was a time of great unrest in the world of humankind. But the life of the forest lived apart from the turmoil as it always had from time immemorial. In these forests of the Holy Land, there were many ancient stands of trees. They watched and witnessed - sometimes for more than a millennium -as the Earth breathed and birthed and buried the endless life forms created by the hand of God.

Among the Cypress, the Elm and the Pine, there was a family of Oak which formed almost a perfect circle. Some were massive - the old ones - these were the sentinels. So tall were they, their sight extended far beyond their sylvan boundaries. Indeed, it is said, they could see into the very hearts of men.

Nestled among its protective kin was 'the Little One', the youngest of the family of Oak. Now small is a relative term for the tree was already ten feet high.

Young trees frolic and play, not unlike the young of every species. And The Little One was no exception. The rabbits, the fox, the wild boar and squirrels scampered beneath the mighty trees. The Little One sent out invitations through its roots and branches and leaves to the more earthbound creatures to hide and climb and share its sights. And the birds nested in its branches, aloft in a sea of green. But the little tree had a restless soul.

"Mother," said The Little One, "am I destined to be one of the Ancient Ones?"

"Is that your wish my Little One?" asked the Mother Oak.

"Yes, Mother, I wish to be able to see to the end of the forest, to the desert, and all the way to the sea! O Mother, wouldn't it be grand to look upon the waves? The winds when they comb through my branches bring the taste and smell of the Deep. The rain tells me stories of the clouds and all the ships they can see. The world is so immense; I wish to see it all!"

The Mother tree laughed. Her heart was full of love for the little tree.

"My, you are adventurous. Only Mother Earth knows our destiny; but you will grow strong and wise as your kin. You come from long - lived stock."

"Does that mean I will see more of the world than any other Oak ever? I so wish for that!"

At that, the Most Wise of the Massive Ancient Oaks spoke.

"Little One, the forest offers peace and safety. It brings the beauty of reflection and the happy litany of time. The most powerful of men, the greatest of monarchs, even Caesar himself, cannot achieve what we claim as our birthright. Do not take this lightly!" The Little One listened with respect, its impatience hidden from the Wise One.

"I know of these gifts; I live them every day. But I wish to see into the hearts of men as you do; to know the rush and buzz of life not rooted to the forest floor."

"Here is baby fox anxious to play. Have a happy heart. And be patient. Trees know patience more than almost almost any other being," said the Mother Oak.

"I'm not bragging, well, perhaps I am. I think it can easily be claimed that we are the most patient and long-lived of all," opined the huge Rock upon which the Mother tree partially stood.

"That is so," agreed the Mother Oak. "We all have our strengths, even the Humans."

Said the Wise One, "I do not wish to speak of Humans. Today they betray their destiny!"

Suddenly, the forest came alive with concern. The moss, trees of all kinds, the birds, the animals, the plants and flowers, and even the earth itself stirred. The Sod beneath the Rock spoke, "Wise One, it has been many hundreds of human years since we have heard you bring such disturbing tidings. What do you mean to say?"

"I will say no more today. Let us all be steady in who we know ourselves to be. We are needed to hold the balance. It is about to be shattered!"

The Wise One sighed and was silent. No one dared to speak further.

CHAPTER II

THE PRELATE

The business of the Roman Empire reached far and wide -
into many foreign lands and cultures. Keeping order among
the people of these provinces was a constant challenge. The
people resented being ruled by strangers and they fought
among themselves to seize what little control they were
allowed.

Pontius Pilate was the Roman prelate in the land of Judea.
The people he ruled over included the Jews and the
Samaritans. He was accountable for the peace to Caesar, the
Roman Emperor. The Romans believed in many gods; the
Jews believed in only One God. They waited for the Messiah,
the son of the True God, of whom their scriptures had
foretold.

Pilate lived in Caesarea, but traveled to neighboring Jerusalem
and the surrounding towns to oversee the Jewish rituals and
festivals, the collection of the taxes and other affairs of state.

He worked with the Sanhedrin, the interpreters and protectors of the Jewish faith and customs, and their high priest, Caiaphas. He had to keep the Jew and the Samaritans in line and, at the same time, ensure that Caesar's rule was unquestioned. His job, perhaps even his life, depended upon the success of this balance. It strained his nerves and made him weary.

When he had the chance, he would go off to the forest and escape the toil and tension. He was especially fond of a stand of Oak deep in the wood. Here he would lie on his back and admire the majestic trees.

"Surely," he thought to himself, "the hand of the gods is at work here. What act of man, whether Caesar's or the most accomplished artisan, could match the perfection of what I now behold?"

It reminded him of his days as a boy in the forests of the North. He missed the green glades and the swirling mists. He took comfort here and often he would fall asleep. He always woke refreshed. His guards knew to leave him undisturbed. It was his secret place.

But lately, he had been deeply troubled. "The Sanhedrin," he grumbled to himself, "are as demanding and unreasonable as Caesar himself."

They were complaining mightily about a Jewish preacher, a prophet, some said, who spoke of the Jews' true God. He claimed to be related by blood to this God. Indeed, he provoked the Sanhedrin's fury by claiming to be this true God's son.

"What foolishness, really," Pilate thought. "Why does it matter whether there is one or many gods? These mighty Oak thrive in their glory nonetheless. If one man believes he is anointed by the hand of his God - what of it? This preacher, whom they call Jesus, appears to be a man of peace. He has organized no armies, he carries not a sword. He aspires to no worldly goods. He is a simple Nazarene, the son of a carpenter. He is no threat to Caesar, nor to me. In these troubled times, is it not good to speak of peace?"

He roused himself, mounted his horse and rode reluctantly out of the forest. His guard, Marcus, waited on his steed at the forest's edge. He greeted Pilate.

"Are you now a new man?" asked Marcus.

"For a moment I was; but this Jesus business washes over me like a stinging desert wind. Have I not enough real trouble without another power play by Caiaphas? I tell you I sometimes believe that man is unhinged! He sees assaulting spirits where there are only men!"

"Yes, Pontius Pilate, here I must agree. I hear talk of trouble concerning this man, Jesus."

"Well, enough then. Let us return home." He looked forward to seeing his good wife, Claudia Procula. Her wise counsel and gentle ways were often a tonic for his stress.

CHAPTER III

THE BETRAYAL

Herod Agrippa, the King of these lands, was not happy with Pontius Pilate. How dare he toss the false Messiah fray in his lap. This man, Jesus, lifted not his little finger to protect himself. Any political fall-out would not be his.

"Send this rabbi back to Pontius Pilate. Even Caiaphas must see that this man is a weak excuse for a warrior seeking to be king. My time would be better spent gossiping by the well."

And so it was that Jesus came again before the Sanhedrin and, though Pilate tried his best to avoid it, before him as well. After much discussion, the Sanhedrin demanded that Jesus be put to death for crimes against Roman and Jewish Law.

"This man will not deny that he is the King of the Jews. He told the Roman tax collectors to leave their posts and follow him. Is this not sedition?" asked Caiaphas.

Pontius Pilate looked upon Jesus whose eyes were clear and very deep: Pilate saw mystery within them which made him all the more uncomfortable.

He asked, "Do you truly believe that you are the king of the Jews?"

Jesus looked with quietude and assurance at Pilate. Pilate read his face to try to find some pride or impudence, but it was not there. Jesus simply replied,

   "It is as you have said it."

The crowd that had gathered roared; the Sanhedrin were outraged. "The last thing I need is to have this spin out of control; I will not put this man to death. They will be content if I offer them the murderer Jesus Barabbas in his place." For it was a custom at Passover to free a prisoner.

But this created confusion. For Jesus Barabbas' name actually meant, 'the son of the father'. The crowd was filled with loyalists of the Sanhedrin. But there were also followers of Jesus, the Rabbi. It sounded like the crowd shouted to release Barabbas. Or did they? Pilate did not know what to do.

"One thing I know; this crowd must be subdued. My garrisons cannot control them if they riot."

"For whom do they call to be released?" he asked Caiaphas.

"Can you not hear them? They ask that you release Barabbas. Jesus must be crucified! They will accept nothing less."

Now Pontius Pilate was not usually an unduly fearful man. But his wife Claudia's dream about Jesus' innocence and his own assessment of the man fought against this outcome.

Again he looked at Jesus. Jesus raised his head and their eyes met.

Thought Pilate, "This man is a mystic; any fool can see that."

He asked Jesus wordlessly:

"If you are the Son of God can you not read my mind? Will you not save yourself?"

Just then, a follower of Jesus thrust himself before Pilate. His name was Joseph of Arimathea. He pleaded:

"Pontius Pilate, this rabbi reveals only God's truth that is in men's hearts! Can you not spare him?" Pilate turned briefly towards Joseph and again back at Jesus. For a long moment he looked into Jesus' face for some response.

And once more he sent his thoughts to Jesus without speaking. "Will you not utter these words of truth to save your own life?" Jesus shook his head no.

Stunned and confused, Pilate replied to Joseph, to Jesus and to his own self:

"What is truth?" He was done with this. He turned to Caiaphas, "This man's blood is upon you. I wash my hands of his execution."

And so it came to pass that Jesus, the prophet of peace and Son of God, was sentenced to be crucified.

CHAPTER IV

THE SOLDIERS

"Servius," called the soldier over his shoulder as he trotted ahead, "this assignment must be done perfectly. Quintus, the executioner, made it clear that he'll have our heads if we don't bring back the perfect tree for the big event."

"Of this I am well aware," replied Servius as he steered the horse and open wagon towards the forest.

"Why all the fuss I do not know for I am a simple soldier. But I tell you, Lucius, the politics this has stirred up is something I want no part of."

"I am with you on that my friend. Let us be about this sorry business with dispatch."

At that the two men entered the woods, startling the silence with the heavy hoofs of the horses and the jangling of the wagon.

Now it was most unusual to send these kinds of soldiers to cut down trees. Normally, this would be the task of the woodsmen. But Quintus had been told in no uncertain terms that this crucifix must be just so. The prisoner, Jesus, must have the very best because he claimed to be a king.

Lucius was intelligent and had a refined sense of beauty. He knew almost as much about trees as the loggers. His father had been one of the most respected woodsmen of his time. As a boy, he had worked by his father's side. While he scanned the forest for the perfect tree, he thought about the nervousness he had seen in Quintus' eyes. He wondered from how far up the chain of command this directive had come.

The Wise One knew the answer and he was afraid. And he was not alone.

"We will not disgrace our lineage," said the Ancient Cedar.

"Nor will we," cried the Elder Pine. "We must all withdraw our energy so that they pass our families by."

The Wise One said to his circle of Oak: "This is what I spoke of."

"Today a member of this forest is destined to be cut down; this is sad. But what is unthinkable is that this tree will be the instrument upon which the Child of God will be murdered."

The forest sighed in sorrow—the trees, the animals, the flowers, the earth itself—with a single voice.

"But Mother, why?" asked the little tree in fear.

"I cannot say, Little One. But now be as still as the rock beneath my roots; pull your energy in. Be more quiet then you have ever been. This is no time for questions." They could sense the thrashing of the wagon against the forest floor. It was getting closer.

Said the Elder Elm: "Till the ends of time this stain will be upon the unlucky tree and its kind. You all know how to honor the silence. Do it now!" The soldiers rumbled towards the Elm. "What about this one, Lucius?" asked Servius pointing to a twenty foot Elm.

"No, it is not right. Let's keep looking."

The soldiers left the stand of Elm; and if the Elm could have they would have collapsed with relief.

The squirrels and the ravens were the lookouts; they watched the progress of the soldiers and, as they made their way through the forest, they passed on what they saw.

"They are coming toward the Cedar stand," cried the Raven. But they did not pause at the Cedar stand. Lucius was looking ahead to the family of Pine who were transfixed with fear.

"There's a noble tree if ever I saw one," said Servius pointing to a strong and sturdy Pine.

"It is true," replied Lucius, "but it is not as Quintus would say, 'just so'. Let us continue."

"They approach," warned the squirrel.

"Yes," said the Wise One. "Be still!" breathed he to his family.

The Mother Oak felt the soldiers coming. She said to the Little One, "Not even a thought, not a question!"

But the Little Tree had many questions. Why would humankind want to kill the Child of the Creator?

"Was this even possible," wondered the Little One. "If one is the Son of the Creator, would his father let him die?"

"How about this one?" asked Servius. He was pointing to the Mother Tree.

"Not my Mother!" cried the Little One at the soldiers. With every bit of energy in its being it declared, "You will not take my mother!"

"Silence!" thundered the Wise One.

"No," replied Lucius, "that Oak is much too big. But this tree looks to be about perfect." He was pointing at the Little One. Without a moment's hesitation, they took their saws and hatchets out and set upon the little tree.

"Oh my Little One, oh no!" cried the Mother Tree. Her heart was severed with every swing of the ax.

It is said that when a tree is cut down that it faints. In what seemed like an instant the Little One had been felled. The soldiers rolled the tree onto the wagon with pulleys and tied it down. They hurried back to Jerusalem.

When they arrived at the executioner's, the carpenters cut the Little One and carved out the two pieces that would form the cross. They hammered the nails into the wood to secure the two pieces. They were in a great rush as the call had come for them to bring the crucifix to where Jesus was. He was about to be released to the crowd cheering for his death.

Simon of Cyrene, who had just come from the hillside, was trying to get a look at Jesus as the crowds whirled around him and the soldiers and high priests pushed him forward.

"Over here, be quick about it," said Gaius, the Centurion, the soldier in charge, to the carpenters. They dropped the little tree, now a cross, on the dusty road.

"We're not carrying this, I can tell you that."

"Seize him!" he said to his soldiers motioning them towards Simon.

"You, you look like a devoted follower of the Nazarene, you carry his cross!" Simon resisted, but it was no use. The soldiers hoisted the cross onto his back and brought him up behind Jesus. The crowd was loud and

Gaius was trying to manage the chaos; all the soldiers were tense.

The Little One, although cut apart, still had consciousness. It was aware of the hardness of the bumpy, rutted road and the softness of Simon's back. So these were the Humans; even the mad dogs that ranged through the forest were not as frightening and wild as these people! Trees sense bloodlust as do all creatures; but this was wanton. It was not killing for food, but for madness!

Though its thoughts were foggy - as the Little Tree was in shock and fading away - still all of this amazed it.

"And I wanted to know more of mankind and their world. I wish with all my heart that I could be back by my Mother's side to see the beauty and the joy of my home again."

Finally, Jesus was brought to Calvary to the hill of Golgotha, which means the place of the skull. There were already two other crosses in place and tied to them were two thieves. There was an area in the middle where they brought Jesus.

The soldiers took the cross and laid it on the ground. They pushed Jesus down onto it and began to drive nails through his hands and into the cross. Jesus cried out in pain. So did the Little Tree. But no one could hear its cries. They were not just of pain for, in truth, the Little One could not feel that much anymore. It was the pain of shame and terrible remorse that speared its soul.

Now, one might question whether a tree or any non-human life form could have a soul. Is a tree really capable of compassion or, for that matter, any noble emotion? After the shock and pain subsided and the crucifix, for that was what the Tree had now become, was placed upright and firmly planted in the ground, the Little One realized that it had no pain at all. The places where Jesus' body touched the tree felt light as air.

Hours passed; the Centurion and his soldiers kept Jesus' followers and the curious crowds from getting too close to the cross. The Little One sensed the broken heart of Jesus' mother, Mary, who watched her son's agony. "My mother also feels this pain - not only of my loss, but of what I have brought on our family."

Just then, Jesus turned his head to the side and spoke to one of the thieves who was next to him. The thief asked Jesus to forgive him and take him to heaven. And Jesus replied, "This day thou shalt be with me in Paradise"

Oh what the Little One would give for Jesus' pardon.

Again, Jesus turned his head to his side. His face was as close to the cross as he could get it. And, in his mind, he spoke to the Little Tree.

"Have no shame, Little One, for you have done me no harm. Indeed, you have allowed me to fulfill the scriptures by offering your life for me."

The Little Tree's heart was bursting.

"But I have been the instrument of your death. And my family will carry this scar always."

"No, Little Oak! Because of your noble heart, your family will be the heroes of the forest! For you have held me up so that I might return to my Father. And I say to you this day I will return you to your home; and in the soil beneath your Mother's outstretched limbs, you will grow anew. And you will live a long and happy life, for you have touched the hand of God."

"You would do this for a tree of the forest?" asked the Little One in wonder.

"My father's face is reflected in all of Earth's creations. You are blessed by the same God who sent me. Now be at peace."

As the sixth hour approached, the sky darkened. By the ninth hour the earth shook, the wind howled, the crowds quaked and Jesus said, "It is accomplished."

The Little One could feel Jesus' spirit depart. And then, with great relief and a peaceful heart, the tree lost consciousness and it too was gone.

Now the soldiers divided Jesus' garments and Joseph of Arimathea received permission from Pilate to take Jesus' body to be buried. After the body was taken away, the gravediggers took down the cross. They too wanted some token of this strange and important event. They took hatchets and chopped up what was left of the Little Tree and were about to take their share when they heard a whish above their heads.

"What in the name of Zeus is that?" cried one of them as he looked up in alarm. They all raised their heads to see the sky once again dark; but this time it was not from clouds. A hundred ravens rushed at them; the men scattered and dashed for cover. Then came one hundred squirrels and twenty fox. The gravediggers looked around in confusion, afraid to move.

And then, as quickly as they had come, the animals were gone. And so was every last piece of the Little Tree!

CHAPTER V

HOME

Pontius Pilate was greatly agitated. Since Jesus' crucifixion, he had felt fear -unnamed, uncircumscribed, unrelenting. Was this a crisis of conscience? "Surely," he reasoned, "I have followed the duties of my office. And I quelled a potentially devastating uprising. Herod is grateful; Caesar is grateful. And I am happy to be done with it. Then why do I feel such unease?"

"I am simply overtired. And Claudia Procula pricks me with her forebodings. I am a Roman in a land that does not suit my temperament."

"Claudius, bring me my stead. And ready yours. We go to the forest."

Claudius was glad for this command. It meant time to relax and wait by the forest's edge.

Pontius Pilate had been restless and short-tempered these last few days. Maybe his humor would improve with a visit to his beloved sanctuary. He readied the horses. And they rode in silence.

"Wait here!" said Pilate as he dismounted and began his hike.

When he came upon his stand of Oak he looked around in horror. Everything was torn apart. And there was a break in the Stand letting the hot sun stream over him.

"Even this," he cried, tears of bitter surprise filling his eyes, "What fool would destroy such beauty!" He sat in his usual spot and looked up at the trees. But he found no peace here.

"Can one be reproached by a tree? I had no part in this," he said, looking as it happened at the Mother Oak. "You are my sanctuary. And now you are defiled." He lay down on the forest floor and felt the odd stillness that spoke no more of comfort.

He felt despair born of he knew not what. "How is a man's worth measured?" he wondered. "I am a good husband, a good Roman, I pay tribute to the gods. These Jews and their affairs are not my world. It is only business. I have done my job."

He lay there reviewing his life, but he could not reconcile his feelings with the facts. And so, after a tortured time, he arose and left his place of contentment for the last time.

 As if responding to a preordained cue, with Pilate's exit, the life of the forest returned. In a moment snatched from time and space, a swirl of a great healing light swept through the Stand of Oak, and when it had exited, all was as it had been before the soldiers had come.

The Little One was there once more next to it's beloved family. Pure joy burst forth from all the creatures of the forest that day.

 "My sweet beloved," cried the Mother Tree.

Her limbs were enabled by the force of her love and she took her child in her outstretched limbs. "I have been blessed beyond reckoning!" exclaimed the Little One. "And so have we all," boomed the Ancient One with great pride and happiness. "Welcome home, Little Tree. The Earth, through Divine Compassion, has created yet another miracle. There is a new wisdom in the world, sprung from true love and unselfishness!"

Irrepressible even now the Little One asked, "Would this then be called 'heaven on earth', now that we have been part of the Creator's intervention?"

"What do you think, Little One?" asked the Ancient One, knowing that this young tree had been anointed with a wisdom that transcended all that had come before among the Great Oaks

"I believe that whenever any being offers a kindness or loving thought in selflessness that we are in the river of the Infinite. It flows in all times and in all places. When we are one with it, that is heaven."

And so it was that this sylvan glade thrived for generation upon generation. The Little Tree grew to be the wisest and tallest of the Wise Ones.

In fulfillment of its' fervent young wish, it learned to see into the hearts of humankind and to look out over the sea, the sky and the cities.

And the Little Tree saw beyond the struggle, strife and cruelty of the world, the kindness and beauty which Jesus had shown existed in every creature, great and small.

"Surely," exclaimed the Little Tree, now so wise and tall, "I have been blessed beyond measure. For even after two millennia I still feel the body of Jesus the Christ in every fiber of my being. I am full of gratitude beyond my capacity. And this is the mystery and the miracle of Divine Love. Thank you Jesus!"

EPILOGUE

It is said that if one ventures deep into the forests of the Holy Land and is very lucky, he or she will come upon a spot of great peace. It is a journey and a destination open to the pure of heart. They will know it by the presence of a great Stand of Oak.

It is also said that some time after Jesus' crucifixion there was found a remnant of the True Cross which brought great healing to the sick and the dying. As it happened, all of the Little Tree's parts were returned but one. It was carefully dropped in a spot that would later be uncovered for the benefit of future generations. It is rumored to be the very cross upon which is built the Church of the Holy Sepulcher in the Holy Land.

And what of Pontius Pilate? The legend says that he returned to the North and died by his own hand. Of course, this cannot be confirmed by history. The Little Tree and Jesus alone know his fate.

www.ingramcontent.com/pod-product-compliance
Lightning Source LLC
Chambersburg PA
CBHW060604030426
42337CB00019B/3605